Copyright 2017 by Philip M. Hudson.
The book author retains sole copyright
to his contributions to this book.

Published 2017.
Printed in the United States of America.

All rights reserved.

No portion of this book may be reproduced, stored in a retrieval system, or transmitted in any form or by any means – electronic, mechanical, photocopy, recording, scanning, or other – except for brief quotations in critical reviews or articles, without the prior written permission of the author.

ISBN 978-1-943650-51-4

Library of Congress Control Number 2017940060

Illustrations – Google Images.

This book may be ordered from
online bookstores.

Published by BookCrafters
Parker, Colorado.
www.bookcrafters.net

Muddy, Muddy

(Children of The Lord)

The traditional song that we all love,
now with *35 new verses*

by Phil Hudson

A Songbook
for God's children of all ages.

Table of Contents

Forty one Verses[1]..2

Discussion Questions 93

Discussion Question Footnotes 115

The Biblical Story of Noah 117

Simple Piano Accompaniment 123

About the Author...125

---

1. Traditional verses are found on pages 10, 12, 14, 18, 28 & 58.

The people, all over, the land were, so naughty, naughty,

People, all over, the land were, so naughty, naughty,

Pride and wealth just….made them haughty, haughty,

Children…..of the Lord.

So rise, and shout, and give God, the glory, glory,

Rise, and shout, and give God, the glory, glory,

Rise and shout and….give God the glory, glory,

Children…..of the Lord.

The whole world, made fun of, made fun of, the prophet, prophet,

Whole world, made fun of, made fun of, the prophet, prophet,

Spirit tried to.....tell them to stop it, stop it,

Children.....of the Lord.

So rise, and shout, and give God, the glory, glory,

Rise, and shout, and give God, the glory, glory,

Rise and shout and….give God the glory, glory,

Children…..of the Lord.

His neighbors, would not turn, would not turn, from sinning, sinning,

Neighbors, would not turn, would not turn, from sinning, sinning,

Though lost, they thought.....that they were winning, winning,

Children.....of the Lord.

So rise, and shout, and give God, the glory, glory,

Rise, and shout, and give God, the glory, glory,

Rise and shout and.....give God the glory, glory,

Children.....of the Lord.

They danced and, they played on, and partied, 'til morning, morning,

Danced and, they played on, and partied, 'til morning, morning,

Noah gave them.....a forewarning, warning,

Children.....of the Lord.

So rise, and shout, and give God, the glory, glory,

Rise, and shout, and give God, the glory, glory,

Rise and shout and….give God the glory, glory,

Children….of the Lord.

The Lord, told Noah, there's gonna be, a floody, floody,

Lord, told Noah, there's gonna be, a floody, floody,

Get those children…..out of the muddy, muddy,

Children…..of the Lord.

So rise, and shout, and give God, the glory, glory,

Rise, and shout, and give God, the glory, glory,

Rise and shout and….give God the glory, glory,

Children…..of the Lord.

Then Noah, he built him, he built him, an Arky, Arky,

Noah, he built him, he built him, an Arky, Arky,

Built it out of....hick·'ry barky, barky,

Children.....of the Lord.

So rise, and shout, and give God, the glory, glory,

Rise, and shout, and give God, the glory, glory,

Rise and shout and….give God the glory, glory,

Children…..of the Lord.

The animals, they came on, they came on, by twosies, twosies,

Animals, they came on, they came on, by twosies, twosies,

Elephants and….kangaroosies, 'roosies,

Children…..of the Lord.

So rise, and shout, and give God, the glory, glory,

Rise, and shout, and give God, the glory, glory,

Rise and shout and….give God the glory, glory,

Children….of the Lord.

The Ark filled with grasses, and apples, and carrots, carrots,

Ark filled with grasses, and apples, and carrots, carrots,

Even bird seed....for hungry parrots, parrots,

Children.....of the Lord.

So rise, and shout, and give God, the glory, glory,

Rise, and shout, and give God, the glory, glory,

Rise and shout and…..give God the glory, glory,

Children…..of the Lord.

It rained, and poured, for for·ty, daisies, daisies,

Rained and it poured, for for·ty daisies, daisies,

Nearly drove those…..animals crazy, crazy,

Children…..of the Lord.

So rise, and shout, and give God, the glory, glory,

Rise, and shout, and give God, the glory, glory,

Rise and shout and…..give God the glory, glory,

Children…..of the Lord.

The lightning, and thunder, they tore things, asunder, 'sunder,

Lightning, and thunder, they tore things, asunder, 'sunder,

All the earth was…..going under, under,

Children…..of the Lord.

So rise, and shout, and give God, the glory, glory,

Rise, and shout, and give God, the glory, glory,

Rise and shout and…..give God the glory, glory,

Children…..of the Lord.

The wicked, who stayed back, did not catch, the boatsy, boatsy,

Wicked, who stayed back, did not catch, the boatsy, boatsy,

Flood came; they thought…..that they could floatsy, floatsy,

Children….of the Lord.

So rise, and shout, and give God, the glory, glory,

Rise, and shout, and give God, the glory, glory,

Rise and shout and.....give God the glory, glory,

Children.....of the Lord.

The whole earth, went under, went under the waters, waters.

Whole earth, went under, went under, the waters, waters,

Covered all God's…..sons and daughters, daughters,

Children…..of the Lord.

So rise, and shout, and give God, the glory, glory,

Rise, and shout, and give God, the glory, glory,

Rise and shout and….give God the glory, glory,

Children….of the Lord.

The family of Noah, kept checking, the weather, weather,

Family of Noah, kept checking, the weather, weather,

Floated for what…..seemed like forever, ever,

Children…..of the Lord.

So rise, and shout, and give God, the glory, glory,

Rise, and shout, and give God, the glory, glory,

Rise and shout and....give God the glory, glory,

Children.....of the Lord.

The sunshine, came out, and dried up, the landy, landy,

Sunshine, came out, and dried up, the landy, landy,

Summer weather…..was very handy, handy,

Children…..of the Lord.

So rise, and shout, and give God, the glory, glory,

Rise, and shout, and give God, the glory, glory,

Rise and shout and….give God the glory, glory,

Children…..of the Lord.

Baptized, by water, the earth was, now ready, ready,

Baptized, by water, the earth was, now ready, ready,

Noah's Ark was…..nice and steady, steady,

Children…..of the Lord.

So rise, and shout, and give God, the glory, glory,

Rise, and shout, and give God, the glory, glory,

Rise and shout and.....give God the glory, glory,

Children.....of the Lord.

The land filled, with new life, that worshipped, the Lordy, Lordy,

Land filled, with new life, that worshipped, the Lordy, Lordy,

Took a flood to…..make a smorgasboardy,

Children…..of the Lord.

So rise, and shout, and give God, the glory, glory,

Rise, and shout, and give God, the glory, glory,

Rise and shout and….give God the glory, glory,

Children…..of the Lord.

No more flooding, from heaven, to start the, world over, over,

Flooding, from heaven, to start the, world over, over,

God gave rainbows…..and four-leaf clover, clover,

Children…..of the Lord. .

So rise, and shout, and give God, the glory, glory,

Rise, and shout, and give God, the glory, glory,

Rise and shout and…..give God the glory, glory,

Children…..of the Lord.

The bow in, the sky was, the Lord's bril·liant promise, promise,

Bow in, the sky was, the Lord's bril·liant promise, promise,

No more sea·sick….hip·popotamuses,

Children….of the Lord.

So rise, and shout, and give God, the glory, glory,

Rise, and shout, and give God, the glory, glory,

Rise and shout and.....give God the glory, glory,

Children.....of the Lord.

Then Noah, he sent out, He sent out, a dovey dovey,

Noah, he sent out, He sent out, a dovey dovey,

Flew all over…..the skies abovey, 'bovey,

Children…..of the Lord.

So rise, and shout, and give God, the glory, glory,

Rise, and shout, and give God, the glory, glory,

Rise and shout and…..give God the glory, glory,

Children…..of the Lord.

The Ark came, to rest on, the tops of, the mountains, mountains,

Ark came, to rest on, the tops of, the mountains, mountains,

No lakes, streams, or…..even fountains, fountains,

Children…..of the Lord.

So rise, and shout, and give God, the glory, glory,

Rise, and shout, and give God, the glory, glory,

Rise and shout and....give God the glory, glory,

Children....of the Lord.

The animals, they walked off, they walked off, by threesies threesies,

Animals, they walked off, they walked off, by threesies threesies,

Koala bears and....chim·pan·zeesies, 'zeesies,

Children.....of the Lord.

So rise, and shout, and give God, the glory, glory,

Rise, and shout, and give God, the glory, glory,

Rise and shout and…..give God the glory, glory,

Children…..of the Lord.

Their new home, on dry ground, was not bought, with money, money,

New home, on dry ground, was not bought, with money, money,

It was flowing…..with milk and honey, honey,

Children…..of the Lord.

So rise, and shout, and give God, the glory, glory,

Rise, and shout, and give God, the glory, glory,

Rise and shout and.....give God the glory, glory,

Children.....of the Lord.

As raindrops, from heaven, go splashing, and splatter, splatter,

Raindrops, from heaven, go splashing, and splatter, splatter,

Think of things that.....really matter, matter.

Children.....of the Lord.

So rise, and shout, and give God, the glory, glory,

Rise, and shout, and give God, the glory, glory,

Rise and shout and....give God the glory, glory,

Children....of the Lord.

They planted, their orchards, with thanks to, their Father, Father,

Planted, their orchards, with thanks to, their Father, Father,

Blessed by His love…..it was no bother, bother,

Children…..of the Lord.

So rise, and shout, and give God, the glory, glory,

Rise, and shout, and give God, the glory, glory,

Rise and shout and....give God the glory, glory,

Children....of the Lord.

His vineyards, and orchards, and gardens, were booming, booming,

Vineyards, and orchards, and gardens, were booming, booming,

Ev'ry-thing was.....alive and blooming, blooming,

Children.....of the Lord.

So rise, and shout, and give God, the glory, glory,

Rise, and shout, and give God, the glory, glory,

Rise and shout and…..give God the glory, glory,

Children…..of the Lord.

We'll go tell, the people, all over, the worldy, worldy,

Go tell, the people, all over, the worldy, worldy,

Tell it to each....boy and girlsy, girlsy,

Children.....of the Lord.

So rise, and shout, and give God, the glory, glory,

Rise, and shout, and give God, the glory, glory,

Rise and shout and…..give God the glory, glory,

Children…..of the Lord.

So give to, our Father, in Heaven, the glory, glory,

Give to, our Father, in Heaven, the glory, glory,

Knock on doors and....tell the story, story,

Children....of the Lord.

So rise, and shout, and give God, the glory, glory,

Rise, and shout, and give God, the glory, glory,

Rise and shout and….give God the glory, glory,

Children….of the Lord.

We've all learned, from Noah, a straight-for·ward, lesson, lesson,

All learned, from Noah, a straight-for·ward, lesson, lesson,

No more sinning.....no more transgression, 'gression,

Children....of the Lord.

So rise, and shout, and give God, the glory, glory,

Rise, and shout, and give God, the glory, glory,

Rise and shout and....give God the glory, glory,

Children....of the Lord.

If you get, to heaven, before, I do·sy, do·sy,
You get, to heaven, before, I do·sy, do·sy,
Tell those ani·mals…..I'm comin' too·sy, too·sy,
Children…..of the Lord.

So rise, and shout, and give God, the glory, glory,

Rise, and shout, and give God, the glory, glory,

Rise and shout and....give God the glory, glory,

Children.....of the Lord.

When I live, in heaven, I'll do some·thing dandy, dandy,

I live, in heaven, I'll do some·thing dandy, dandy,

Drill a hole and…..grab your handy, handy,

Children…..of the Lord.

So rise, and shout, and give God, the glory, glory,

Rise, and shout, and give God, the glory, glory,

Rise and shout and.....give God the glory, glory,

Children.....of the Lord.

One day, we, will go and, we'll live with, God's creatures, creatures,

One day, we'll go and, we'll live with, God's creatures, creatures,

All those who have.....angelic features, features,

Children.....of the Lord.

So rise, and shout, and give God, the glory, glory,

Rise, and shout, and give God, the glory, glory,

Rise and shout and….give God the glory, glory,

Children…..of the Lord.

From rhinos, to lizards, to big arm·adillos 'dillos,

Rhinos, to lizards, to big, arm·adillos 'dillos,

Cater·pillars…..on leafy pillows, pillows,

Children…..of the Lord.

So rise, and shout, and give God, the glory, glory,

Rise, and shout, and give God, the glory, glory,

Rise and shout and....give God the glory, glory,

Children....of the Lord.

There'll be puppies, and kittens, and all kinds, of turtles, turtles,

Puppies, and kittens, and all kinds, of turtles, turtles,

We'll have fun with…..monkeys and gerbils, gerbils,

Children…..of the Lord.

So rise, and shout, and give God, the glory, glory,

Rise, and shout, and give God, the glory, glory,

Rise and shout and….give God the glory, glory,

Children….of the Lord.

There'll be eagles, and beagles, and otters, and beavers, beavers,

Eagles, and beagles, and otters, and beavers, beavers,

There'll be room for…..golden retrievers, 'trievers,

Children…..of the Lord.

So rise, and shout, and give God, the glory, glory,

Rise, and shout, and give God, the glory, glory,

Rise and shout and....give God the glory, glory,

Children....of the Lord.

The tiger, and cheetah, and leopard, and lion, lion,

Tiger, and cheetah, and leopard, and lion, lion,

All the ani·mals…..you'd find in Zion, Zion,

Children…..of the Lord.

So rise, and shout, and give God, the glory, glory,

Rise, and shout, and give God, the glory, glory,

Rise and shout and….give God the glory, glory,

Children….of the Lord.

The pandas, and possums, are waiting, in heaven, heaven,

Pandas, and possums, are waiting, in heaven, heaven,

There to wel·come.....all of their brethren, brethren,

Children.....of the Lord.

So rise, and shout, and give God, the glory, glory,

Rise, and shout, and give God, the glory, glory,

Rise and shout and....give God the glory, glory,

Children.....of the Lord.

God's angels, in heaven, will heal every, creature, creature,

Angels, in heaven, will heal every, creature, creature,

Guide us to our…..devoted Teacher, Teacher,

Children…..of the Lord.

So rise, and shout, and give God, the glory, glory,

Rise, and shout, and give God, the glory, glory,

Rise and shout and….give God the glory, glory,

Children…..of the Lord.

We'll live in His kingdom, for all time, forever, ever,

Live in, His kingdom, for all time, forever ever,

With our friends we'll…..be together, 'gether,

Children…..of the Lord.

So rise, and shout, and give God, the glory, glory,

Rise, and shout, and give God, the glory, glory,

Rise and shout and....give God the glory, glory,

Children.....of the Lord.

At bedtime, we'll drift off, to sleep, with the story, story,

Bedtime, we'll drift off, to sleep with, the story, story,

Dream·ing will be....hunky dory, dory,

Children.....of the Lord.

So rise, and shout, and give God, the glory, glory,

Rise, and shout, and give God, the glory, glory,

Rise and shout and….give God the glory, glory,

Children….of the Lord.

So rise, and shine, and wait for, the Rapture, Rapture,

Rise, and shine, and wait for, the Rapture, Rapture,

Let God seek your.....soul to capture, capture,

Children.....of the Lord.

So rise, and shout, and give God, the glory, glory,

Rise, and shout, and give God, the glory, glory,

Rise and shout and….give God the glory, glory,

Children…..of the Lord.

Now this is, the end of, the end of, our story, story,

This is, the end of, the end of, our story, story,

There just isn't.....any morey, morey,

Children.....of the Lord.

So rise, and shout, and give God, the glory, glory,

Rise, and shout, and give God, the glory, glory,

Rise and shout and....give God the glory, glory,

Children....of the Lord.

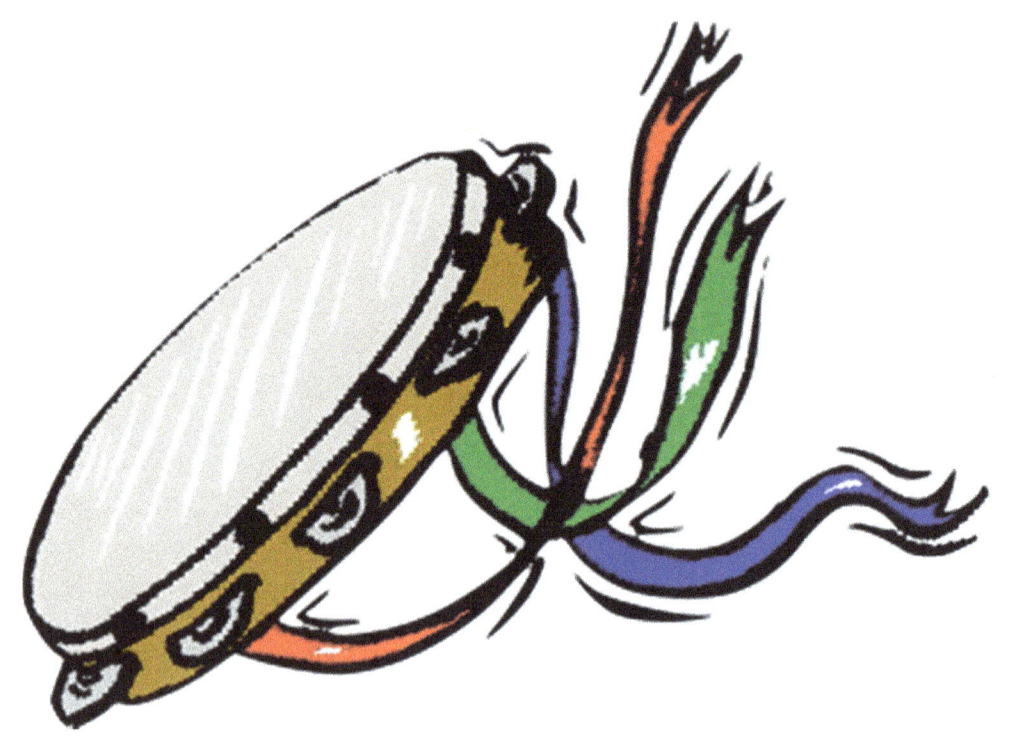

"Choose you this day whom ye will serve, but as for me and my house, we will serve the Lord." (Joshua 24:15).

"Come now,
and let us reason together."
(Isaiah 1:18).

(food for thought)

One Hundred Discussion Questions

1. Why do you think the people all over the land were so naughty in the days of Noah?

2. How was Noah sure that he was preaching the word of the Lord?

3. Why do you think the Lord chose Noah, from among all of His children, to carry His message to the world?

4. Today, to whom does the Lord speak?

5. Why wouldn't the people listen to the prophet when he urged them to repent?

6. Why did Noah's neighbors take pleasure in sin?

7. How do you think the devil was able to carefully lead the people down the road to hell?

8. How do you think Noah must have felt when his neighbors rejected his invitation to repent?

9. Today, in what ways do wicked people make fun of the prophet, compared to how Noah was treated?

10. Why would the Spirit stop striving with Noah's wicked neighbors?

11. It hadn't started raining when God commanded Noah to build the Ark. In fact, there might not have been a cloud in the sky. How do you think this made Noah feel when he started gathering together all the supplies he would need for his Ark-building project?

12. Where do you think Noah learned how to build the Ark?

13. Do you think God provided him with detailed plans?

14. Do you think that Noah might have been able to do it on his own without God's help?

15. Do you know how long Noah prepared for the Flood, before it actually started raining?

16. Why would it be important for Noah to stock up on food, toothpaste, dramamine, and bathroom tissue beforehand?

17. How do you think the animals knew that they should board the Ark?

18. Do you think that Noah and the animals were able to speak to each other?

19. If animals could speak to you, what do you think they might say?

20. Do you think the animals trusted Noah?

21. Do you think the elephants caused the Ark to tip, or to dangerously rock back and forth, when they came on board?

22. Do you think the swans and geese would have needed life vests?

23. It must have been hectic when it was time to enter the Ark. Do you think the animals all got along with each other during the boarding process?

24. Do you think they treated each other kindly?

25. What do you think all of the people who had not listened to Noah did, when it started to rain?

26. How do you think they felt? Do you think they suddenly had a desire to repent?

27. Do you think it was too late for them to do so?

28. What do you think happened to all the gold, silver, and other treasures that had been hoarded by those who had been left behind, when the Ark floated away?

29. Do you think that some of the people might have had second thoughts?

30. Do you think they might have offered Noah all of their worldly goods in exchange for passage on the Ark?

31. Why do you think God would have decided to send a flood, in the first place?

32. At the creation of the world, God had pronounced everything He had made as "good," or "very good." What do you think happened to change that?

33. What do you think the Flood symbolizes? What does the Flood mean to you?

34. Why do you think Noah wouldn't let his wicked neighbors board the Ark, after it started raining?

35. How do you think Noah felt when it rained for 40 straight days? Do you think he might have thought, just for a moment, that he was in Portland, Oregon?

36. What do you think the animals drank and ate while they were on the Ark?

37. Do you think Noah and his family might have enjoyed fresh milk each morning?

38. How about scrambled eggs for breakfast? How about bacon? Or hamburgers? Or honey on their biscuits?

39. How do you think they could see at night? Do you think there were fireflies?

40. Do you think that the rhinos and giraffes were more comfortable on the ark than the ducks and loons? Why or why not?

41. Do you think the porcupines and skunks might have been given their own special, private quarters?

42. Do you know why the elephants didn't go swimming during the time they spent on the Ark?[1]

43. What kinds of bedtime stories do you think Moses and his family told the animals?[2]

44. Do you think they talked about Goldilocks and the Three Bears?

45. Do you think the animals took baths every night before bed?

46. Do you know what the expression "crow's nest" means?³

47. Did Noah need to worry about hitting any other boats while the Ark bobbed around on the water?

48. Sailing ships have a "poop deck."⁴ Do you think the Ark had one?

49. If there was a poop deck, what do you think Noah and the animals used it for?

50. Do you think there was hydroponic gardening⁵ on the Ark?

51. After it stopped raining, they may have floated around for weeks, or even months. If so, why do you think God would allow them to do so?

52. How did God reveal to Noah that the waters were receding?

53. What sign did God give to Noah that he would never again send a flood upon the earth?

54. Have you ever seen a full rainbow after a storm? How did it make you feel?

55. Do you remember how the air smells after it has rained? Does it smell clean?

56. Have you ever wondered if the earth has a spirit? If so, do you think it might have needed to be baptized, just like you?

57. What does it mean to feel "fine and dandy?"

58. Do you ever feel that God is offering you a fresh start? If so, what can you do now, to "start over?"

59. Have you experienced what it feels like to come up out of the waters of baptism? Do you think the earth might have felt special, too, after the Flood?

60. When the sun finally came out, how do you think Noah and his family felt? Do you think they might have been able to feel the Spirit?

61. Do you think they needed to put on sunscreen?

62. Would you like to share the story of Noah with your friends? What would you tell them?

63. How are some people today like Noah's neighbors before the Flood?

64. How do you think Noah felt having to start life all over again, after the flood? Do you think he got any help from God?

65. Have you ever had to start over, after moving to a new home or a new school?

66. How do you think the story of Noah's Ark glorifies our Father in Heaven?

67. What lessons have you learned from the story of Noah's Ark and the Flood?

68. What do you think it means, that the whole earth worshipped God after the Flood?

69. Why do you think God makes only a few four-leaf clovers? Why is it so special, when you see a rainbow?

70. What do you think Noah taught his family, before, during, and after the Flood? Do you think they discussed some of the same things you and your family talk about?

71. How do you feel when you take care of the earth?

72. Do you know what it means to be given a "stewardship responsibility?"

73. When you see animals in the forest, are you ever reminded of God's love for all of His children?

74. Do puppies or kittens help you to remember that God loves you?

75. Do you think animals go to heaven? If so, which ones?

76. Have you ever wondered if your favorite pet might be waiting for you in heaven? How do you think it might greet you, when you go home to God?

77. Why do you think that animals in heaven might have "angelic features?"

78. Do you think the animals that God created, and put in the Garden of Eden, might have also had "angelic features?"

79. Do you think that the children of the Lord were meant to get along with each other? How about people?

80. How do you think God would like you to show your love for Him?

81. What is your favorite kind of dog? Do you think its ancestors might have been on Noah's Ark?

82. What kinds of animals do you think live in Zion?⁶

83. Do you think animals will get along with each other in heaven as well as their ancestors did when they lived on the Ark?

84. How do you think the family of Noah behaved after they left the Ark? How did God make it possible for His children to live happily ever after?

85. Do you think the story of Noah's Ark might have been one of the world's first fairy tales? What principles of the gospel might the story of Noah symbolize?

86. How has reading stories from scriptures allowed God to "capture your soul?"

87. Can you think of other Bible stories that teach us about God's love for His children?[7]

88. Can you think of any latter-day prophets who remind you of Noah?[8] Can you name them?

89. What have the prophets said that has impressed you?

90. After Noah had been so blessed by the Lord, do you think he ever stopped listening to Him and following His counsel?

91. What do you think it means to have faith in the teachings of the Lord's servants who have been called to the work?

92. Do you think the Lord's prophet would ever lead His people to do things that were not in their best interest?

93. What do you think God meant when He said that Noah was perfect in his generation?

94. Can you think of any ways that you could be "perfect in your generation?"⁹

95. How has God blessed you when you have been obedient?

96. How would you describe your family life, when you obey your elders?

97. What are some of the other things that God would like you to know, about which His prophets have spoken?¹⁰

98. Do you think that it is important to follow the prophets, even when you do not know all of the details relating to their messages?

99. How have you responded in the past to God's instruction that has been directed to you?

100. How do you think your obedience to His counsel makes Him feel? Someday, would you like to meet Noah and all of the animals that were with him on the Ark? What might you want to say to them?

Footnotes:

1. It was because they had only one pair of trunks!

2. It was not Moses, but Noah, who was on the Ark! (Did I fool you?)

3. Ask an adult, and then ask yourself the question: Do you think the Ark might have had a real "crow's nest?"

4. A Poop deck is not what you might think. It's the highest deck at the rear of the ship.

5. Hydroponic gardening the method of growing plants without soil, using mineral nutrient solutions in a water solvent.

6. Zion is where the "pure in heart" live.

7. Think of the Children of Israel leaving Egypt, Moses parting the Red Sea, Daniel in the lion's den, David and Goliath, the widow's cruze of oil, and Jesus feeding the multitude.

8. Joseph Smith, Brigham Young, John Taylor, Wilford Woodruff, Lorenzo Snow, Joseph F. Smith, Heber J. Grant, George Albert Smith, David O. McKay, Joseph Fielding Smith, Harold B. Lee, Spencer W. Kimball, Ezra Taft Benson, Howard W. Hunter, Gordon B. Hinckley, and Thomas S. Monson (as of 2017).

9. Hint: Noah asked his neighbors if they would repent, and then obey the commandments.

10. Think of covenants, ordinances, faith, repentance, baptism, and the Holy Ghost, the temple, the Sabbath, tithing, the Word of Wisdom, and The Book of Mormon.

The Story of Noah in The Old Testament

There are roughly 76 verses in Genesis Chapters 6 - 9 that deal with Noah and the Flood. The following is excerpted from the King James Version of these chapters.

"And God saw that the wickedness of man was great in the earth, and that every imagination of the thoughts of his heart was only evil continually. And the Lord said, I will destroy man whom I have created from the face of the earth; both man, and beast, and the creeping thing, and the fowls of the air; for it repenteth me that I have made them. But Noah found grace in the eyes of the Lord.

God said unto Noah, The end of all flesh is come before me; for the earth is filled with violence through them; and, behold, I will destroy them with the earth. Make thee an ark of gopher wood. And of every living thing of all flesh, two of every sort shalt thou bring into the ark, to keep them alive with thee; they shall be male and female. Thus did Noah; according to all that God commanded him, so did he.

I will cause it to rain upon the earth forty days and forty nights; and every living substance that I have made will I destroy from off the face of the earth. And Noah did according unto all that the Lord commanded him. And it came to pass after seven days, that the waters of the flood were upon the earth. And the waters prevailed, and were increased greatly upon the earth; and the ark went upon the face of the waters. And the waters prevailed exceedingly upon the earth; and all the high hills, that were under the whole heaven, were covered.

And every living substance was destroyed which was upon the face of the ground, both man, and cattle, and the creeping things, and the fowl of the heaven; and they were destroyed from the earth: and Noah only remained alive, and they that were with him in the ark. And the waters prevailed upon the earth an hundred and fifty days.

And the waters returned from off the earth and were abated. And the ark rested upon the mountains of Ararat. Also he sent forth a dove from him, to see if the waters were abated from off the face of the ground. And the dove came in to him in the evening; and, lo, in her mouth was an olive leaf plucked off: so Noah knew that the waters were abated from off the earth. And Noah removed the covering of the ark, and looked, and, behold, the face of the ground was dry.

And Noah went forth, and every beast, every creeping thing, and every fowl, and whatsoever creepeth upon the earth, after their kinds, went forth out of the ark.

And the Lord said in his heart, I will not again curse the ground any more for man's sake. And God blessed Noah and his sons, and said unto them, Be fruitful, and multiply, and replenish the earth. And God said, I do set my bow in the cloud, and it shall be for a token of a covenant between me and the earth. And

it shall come to pass that the bow shall be seen in the cloud. And Noah began to be an husbandman, and he planted a vineyard."

Singing together is fun!

How many verses have you been able to memorize?

Muddy, Muddy

About the Author

Phil Hudson and Jan, his wife of 49 years, have 7 children and over 20 grandchildren. They enjoy spending time with their family at their cabin nestled in the Selkirk Mountains, on the shore of Priest Lake, the crown jewel of North Idaho. Phil has been singing to his kids and grandkids at bedtime for nearly half a century and has no plans to let up.